How to Memorize Bible Scriptures and Verses

Quickly and Easily

By Brian Gugas (Author)

Print Edition

Copyright 2015 Brian Gugas. All Rights Reserved. No part of this publication may be reproduced, distributed or transmitted in any form or by any means, or stored in a database or retrieval system, without the prior written permission of the publisher.

Disclaimer: *This book contains general information that is based on author's own knowledge and experiences. It is published for general reference purposes only. The publisher and the author disclaim any personal liability, either directly or indirectly, for the information contained within. Although the author and the publisher have made every effort to ensure the accuracy and completeness of the information contained within, we* assume no responsibility for errors, inaccuracies, omissions and inconsistencies.

All Scripture quotations, unless otherwise indicated, are taken from the Holy Bible, New International Version®, NIV®. Copyright ©1973, 1978, 1984, 2011 by Biblica, Inc.™ Used by permission of Zondervan. All rights reserved worldwide. www.zondervan.com The "NIV" and "New International Version" are trademarks registered in the United States Patent and Trademark Office by Biblica, Inc.™

Contact the Author:

briangugas@gmail.com

Author Website: *http://briangugas.com*

Dedication:

To my wife and sons,

Through all the Life's Pleasures and Sorrows

Contents

Introduction 1

Get To Know Your Bible 5

What Kind of Learner are YOU 13

Memorize God's Word with your Family 19

Memorize with Other Christians 27

Repeat after Me 33

Write On! 37

More Than Just Words on a Page 45

A Great Place to Start 57

Additional Resources 83

Your Free Gift: 85

Other Books By Brian 87

Your Free Gift:

Thanks for reading my book and as a way of saying Thank You I have this free gift for you.

In Bible Verses and Inspirational Christian Quotes Book, you will have quotes and explanations some very important aspects of our life i.e Friendship, Life, Peace, Motivation, Salvation and many more...

Use this link to get the free gift - http://briangugas.com/free-gift

Introduction

The thought of memorizing verses from the Bible is one that usually terrifies people. They (and possibly you) say things like... "I can't do *that!*" "That's impossible." "I've never been good at memorizing anything." "A lot of those verses don't make sense to me when I read them, so I sure can't memorize them."

Let me ask you this:

- How many songs can you sing from memory?
- How many nursery rhymes can you quote?
- Is it safe to say you passed third grade because you memorized your multiplication facts?
- How do you find your way around town—is it because you've memorized the routes to your favorite places?

- Do you use a recipe for everything you cook?
- What is your address and phone number? Your social security number?
- Do you have to use cheat sheets for your PIN and passwords online?
- Do you have the birthdays of your family members memorized?

But...but...but....you stammer. Those things are important. You have to know those things to navigate life. Well here's a newsflash for you: you need the Word of God to navigate life more than you need all of those other things put together. You need the Word of God to navigate life here on earth in such a way that you spend eternity with God in heaven.

Having key verses of the Bible memorized allows you to have the Word in your heart and mind in times of fear, difficulty, joy, excitement, and frustration. David said in Psalms 119:105, *"Your word is a lamp for my feet and a light on my path..."* So in other words, memorizing Bible verses is a way to grow and mature in your relationship with the LORD.

The purpose of this book is to help you do just that—memorize Bible verses and grow in your relationship with the LORD. The purpose of this book is NOT to make you feel guilty, dumb, or lacking in your love for the LORD. So as you read, do so prayerfully and with an open heart and mind; believing you can memorize God's Word and become more familiar with the Bible.

BRIAN GUGAS

Get To Know Your Bible

As a Christian, we can't really be growing and maturing in our faith if we don't know what the Bible says—what God expects and desires of us, what promises he has made us, how to share our faith, how to function in the church and in the world, and the importance and power of prayer and worship in our lives. Think about it, (most) of us don't try to put a child's bicycle together or assemble furniture from IKEA without reading the directions, so why would we even think about living a Christian life without the very Word of God to show/teach you how?

No, this doesn't mean you have to memorize the Bible from cover to cover but it does mean you need to be familiar with the Bible. In fact, if you aren't familiar with your

Bible, don't worry about memorizing scripture until you are. But what does that mean? What does it mean to be familiar with the Bible? It means you:

- Can find the different books of the Bible with ease and without having to refer to the table of contents (using the finger tabs is 'fair')
- Know the differences between the Old and New Testaments and their significance historically, prophetically, and doctrinally
- Understand the relationship between God and the Israelites and God and the Gentiles

- Understand how and why the Law of Moses is no longer applicable
- Know what is necessary to accept the gift of salvation according to the scriptures rather than man
- Be able to tell the most fundamental Bible stories
- Be able to back up why you believe what you believe with scripture references

As you read through that list, how many of these things do you feel confident about? If someone came to you asking you what the Bible has to say about (fill in the blank), would you be able to answer them and prove your answers by showing them scriptures that validate what you have said? Or would you be able to use a concordance or Bible dictionary to locate verses to do so?

I'll say it again—this is not meant to be a guilt trip. It's meant to be a wake-up call; one that ignites in you a desire to know God's Word more deeply in order that you might live it more fully and share it with others. And don't worry—no one, not even God, expects you to do this overnight or to do it on your own. But you've got to start somewhere, so as the saying goes..."there's no time like the present".

Start here

Becoming familiar with your Bible requires you to:

- Have a Bible
- Read your Bible
- Have an attitude that wants to learn

- Have someone you can go to for help and answers to questions you have—your preacher, Bible school teacher, or a friend or family member who is more mature in their faith
- Highlighters to mark key verses in your Bible
- Notecards, a journal, or post-it notes

Start small

Don't feel you have to do everything at once. Get in the habit of reading from your Bible for a few minutes every day (fifteen minutes or so). I would suggest reading either the book of Psalms, Matthew, or James. As you read don't hesitate to underline or highlight verses that stand out to you and to write down where those verses are found on a separate sheet of paper. Example: Matthew 6:33.

Additionally, don't hesitate to make notes as to questions you have about the Bible in general or what you read. There are also a number of resources available to help you better understand the Bible. A concordance, maps of the Middle East showing where places were /are, books and websites that provide information about when and why each book of the Bible was written are just a few of the things you will find helpful to you.

After you've been reading for a couple of weeks, take a look at the list of verses you've written down and marked in your Bible. Select one or two you feel are especially meaningful to you. *These* are the verses you are going to memorize...first. Trust me, you can do this!

HOW TO MEMORIZE BIBLE SCRIPTURES AND VERSES

What Kind of Learner are YOU

If you have trouble memorizing or even remembering things, chances are you are going about it the wrong way. This is especially true when trying to memorize Bible verses.

Most people think that the only way to memorize a Bible verse is to read it over and over from the Bible until you know what it says. Now while that method works for some, it doesn't work for everyone because not everyone learns or comprehends in the same way.

To help you understand which methods of memorizing will work best for you, let's take a few minutes to help you evaluate your learning style. In doing so, you can avoid feelings of frustration and failure in this and many other things, as well.

The three basic styles of learning

The three basic styles of learning are: VISUAL, AURAL, and TACTILE (hands-on).

Visual learners are those that learn best by reading something, watching instructional videos, and answering questions you read in a workbook or worksheets. Visual learners are those that memorize best by reading and re-reading. They look at it until it is imprinted on their brain.

Aural learners are those that learn best by hearing. They soak up information during lectures, enjoy being read to, and by listening to someone explain how to play a game or put a bicycle together. Audial learners need to hear the Word to memorize it.

Tactile, or hands-on learners, want to do it themselves. They want something they can hold in their hands. Having something tangible gives them the focus they need to accomplish their task.

Do you know what kind of learner you are? Don't worry if you think you lie somewhere in the middle, because from these three basic learning styles comes a more detailed assessment, which you will see described below. So to help you get started in SUCCESSFULLY memorizing Bible verses, take a few minutes to assess which style of learner you are. Once you have, you will be able to choose the method of memorizing that will be the least frustrating and most enjoyable (and successful).

- **Visual learners:** Like to read, are good spellers, have nice handwriting, are detail oriented and would rather watch to see how things are done before attempting something themselves. Visual learners excel by using flash cards, charts, and colorful markers.

- **Aural learners:** Aural learners excel as long as they can hear what is being taught. Aural learners crave conversation, work best with music playing in the background, and by having directions and stories read to them.

- **Verbal learners:** Love words. They excel in reading, writing, speech and debate. Verbal learners are good listeners-they thrive on words-as well as being good story tellers and story writers. They get bored in lectures, though, as they would rather read it for themselves.

- **Tactile learners:** Tactile learners excel in science, cooking, arts and crafts, sports and music. They want to do it themselves and learn best when you allowed to do things in steps- mastering one step before moving on to the next.

- **Logical learners:** Love to reason. They prefer numbers over letters, but will read if it is something they consider relevant and useful.

- **Social learners:** Work best in groups. They aren't necessarily competitive, but need the social interaction and comradery to keep them going.

- **Solitary learners:** Love the peace and quiet when reading or doing most any task. The solitary learner categorizes fun and learning; making time for both, but rarely mixing the two.

Were you able to determine how you learn best? Now let's use that to get you into God's Word and to get God's Word into you.

Memorize God's Word with your Family

Family devotions are NEVER a bad idea. But when you add an element of memorization to it, you can challenge and encourage each other to learn...in a not-too-competitive way, of course.

Memorizing Bible verses as a family is a wonderful way to make God's presence in your home real and genuine. Memorizing as a family also:

- Encourages you to not give up
- Holds you accountable for the commitment you've made to memorize a verse (or verses)
- Brings an added sense of unity to your family

- Allows you to work as a team and not feel so alone in your quest to put God's Word to memory

Don't make it a burden or drudgery, though. Make it fun! Make it enjoyable, and make it easy so no one gets discouraged.

At the dinner table

Say the verse you are working on together at the dinner table a few times while eating. For example, whenever Dad says, "Forks down." it's time to say the verse. Or...once everyone is fairly familiar with the verse, make it a requirement that they have to say it from memory before they get dessert or leave the table.

Write it on their...

Write the verse on a sticky note or note card and put it in your purse, lunch bag, briefcase, or book bag so you will see it throughout the day.

Write the verse in marker or lipstick on the bathroom mirrors of your house.

Write the verse on sticky notes or note cards and put them around the house where you can see them. For example: kitchen cabinets, the dashboard of the car, on the front of the microwave, on the TV remote....

Place a notecard with the verse on everyone's pillow and let it be the last thing they look at each night before going to bed.

And the award goes to...

Reward yourselves when you memorize three or four verses. You can do this on an individual basis or make it a family affair.

When doing it on an individual basis, it is important to remember to strike a balance between rewarding those who have memorized their verses and not making other family members (especially children) feel unaccomplished .NOTE: If doing individual awards, never compare one child's accomplishments to another's.

Some of the individual awards you might offer include:

- A chore-free day
- A later bedtime for a day or two
- Playdate with a friend
- Choosing something to do with just mom or dad
- Choosing the movie for family movie night
- A small gift such as a book, craft kit, trip to the yogurt or ice cream shop,

or something else the person will enjoy NOTE: Moms especially like a few hours of 'me time'

Family rewards could include:

- A special dinner out
- A trip to the zoo or other fun activity
- Making homemade ice cream together
- Staying up late, eating popcorn, and watching a movie together
- A family evening at the bowling alley
- A backyard game night

For all the right reasons

Memorizing Bible verses with your family can sometimes cause us (and especially children) to learn the verses for the sake of 'winning' rather than for putting God's Word into their hearts and minds. You can also avoid the competition mindset between your children by not having that mindset yourself.

Consistency

It is also important to review the verses you've learned from time to time. If you don't you'll forget them; making all that hard work seem like a waste. Reviewing the verses to keep them fresh in your mind is important if you are memorizing for the right reasons—to *know* God's Word, to be able to share the Word with others, and to use God's Word to bring you into a deeper relationship with God.

I have a friend who had memorized numerous Bible verses in her life, but at one point decided she was going to memorize the entire Sermon on the Mount (chapters 5, 6, 7 of Matthew). She memorized it in small sections, but every day before learning more verses, she would say the ones she had already learned.

When she had memorized all three chapters, she made a point to recite it to herself every day while walking. This went on for quite some time. But then she missed a day or two here and there, and do you know what happened? She started to forget *exactly* how some of the verses read. She could still say quite a bit of it word for word, but other parts were not as correct.

You don't learn a song only to never sing it again, do you? The same holds true for memorizing verses from the Bible, too.

Memorize with Other Christians

Proverbs 27:17 says, *As iron sharpens iron, so one man sharpens another.* Having the help and accountability that comes from studying and memorizing with other Christians is a great way to grow and mature in Christ.

Most groups like this will meet once a week for an hour to read, pray, work on memory verses, and enjoy a time of fellowship. In meeting like this, you not only learn by studying and working on memory work together, but you grow in your relationships with you Christian brothers and sisters. Having that bond of friendship makes studying together more meaningful and productive. You develop a sense of trust in one another. You aren't embarrassed or intimidated by each other; making it possible to relax and open your heart and mind to what God's Word has to say to you.

Small group Bible study groups are common in churches today, but those who work together to commit scripture to memory are the groups that have the greatest impact on the lives of those in the group as well as those the group members come in contact with. If you don't believe that, read what Dale has to say...

I've been a Christian most of my life. I'm an elder in the church and enjoy reading my Bible each day. I have no trouble finding passages of scripture I want to share with others or use in a lesson, but I had never memorized any verses. I was sure I couldn't. Not me. But when our preacher asked me to be part of an intense Bible study group that would include memorizing several key Bible verses, I said I would. I was still convinced I'd never be able to do it, but I figured I should at least try.

The group was great. There were eight of us who'd gone to church together for years. I was one of the oldest ones in the group, but I wasn't the only one who was afraid of the memory work. So each week we would pair up and say our verses to each other. It was a little hard for me at first, but after I had memorized a couple of verses, I figured out it wasn't as bad or as hard as I thought it would be.

Our group met together for a little over two years. In that time we memorized about twenty-five Bible verses and studied the Bible more deeply than I ever had before. The group changed my life.

Amanda has this to say about the Bible study/memorization group she was in:

I wasn't sure I even wanted to be a part of the group, but my minister said he really wanted me to do it because I was taking on the responsibility of leading our children's ministry, and part of our curriculum included having the children memorize their weekly Bible verse. It didn't take more than a couple of weeks for me to realize that I enjoyed the challenge of memorizing, the fellowship of the group, and the fact that memorizing God's Word made the verses more meaningful to me. They weren't just words on a page to be read and obeyed. They made me who I am. But I think the most important thing about being in the group was that it made me more capable of sharing God's Word with the children I was teaching and to teach them how to memorize their Bible verses.

How to get involved

- If your church has small-group Bible studies, get involved in one (if you aren't already). If the group doesn't make an effort to memorize scripture, ask the leader if he/she would consider doing so.

- Ask a few people at church if they would be interested in being part of a group like the one Dale described. Once you have a small group of people (6 to 8) ready to dig deeper into the Word, select a book of the Bible to study or a topic that will help you mature in your relationship with God. Look for key verses in the Bible that relate to the book you are studying and commit to memorizing them over the course of your study. Don't overwhelm yourselves, though. Four to six verses is adequate for a group just beginning to memorize Bible verses.

- Start an online scripture memorization group. Social media allows you to send group messages; making it easy to communicate with everyone at one time. These groups do require you to be on an 'honor system' of sorts, as there is no one to actually hear you say your verses from memory.

We worship with our brothers and sisters in Christ. We pray with them, fellowship with them, serve with them, and learn with them. Why not memorize God's Word with them, too?

Repeat after Me

For those who are aural learners (learn by hearing), memorizing scripture by using an audio Bible is often the key to being successful.

Audio Bibles are available in CD format, or as an app for your phone or e-reader. You can listen when you are driving, taking a walk, fixing dinner, or enjoying a bit of quiet time with God.

Another option you have is the voice function on most computers, tablets, and phones that will talk to you; telling you what's on the page. For example, if you were memorizing Hebrews 13:7, you could look it up, use the voice function, and you would hear the verse being read. Some of the most popular apps for this are: MemVerse, RememberMe, and MobilizeFaith.

A lot of the Bible verses I know are the ones I learned as a kid—thanks to the cassette tapes my mom had for us to listen to. Steve Green's "Hide 'em in your Heart" tapes put lots of Bible verses to music. The songs were catchy and easy to learn. He sang some of them, but kids sang most of them, and I remember thinking that was really cool. Before each song they always read the verse from the Bible and told where it was found. I actually still sing these songs because they are so stuck in my head and I'm twenty-seven years old! For example, I recently had a health emergency requiring a lengthy hospital stay. And as is normal procedure, I had to have several IVs and blood draws. I'm not fond of needles, to put it mildly, so every time they had to stick me, I would sing one of those songs in my head: "When I am afraid I will trust in you in God whose word I praise." (Psalm 56: 3). Now that I have a two year-old son, I am going to get them for him. I can download them onto my tablet. I thank God I have parents who cared enough to put God's Word in my heart and mind right from the start. ~Olivia

Scripture verses set to music aren't just for kids—not even if kids are the ones singing. These songs are a wonderful way to memorize. Most people even say it's much easier to memorize scripture when doing it to music. There's just something about singing it that makes it seem less difficult.

If none of these methods of listening for the purpose of memorizing verses from the Bible appeals to you or aren't accessible, you can always ask someone to read the verse to you, or read it aloud to yourself. Take it from an aural learner when I say reading the verse aloud to yourself over and over does work.

Reading verses aloud to others—especially young children—offers the advantage of having someone there to listen as you and your child learns to say the verse from memory. While reading it aloud to yourself doesn't give you that sense of accountability some people need, for many people, just hearing the words makes them easier to remember—even if it is their own voice.

Whether it be set to music, an app on a phone, or just talking to yourself as you study, if speaking God's Word aloud is the most effective way for you to memorize, do it. You will be amazed at the difference it makes in your life.

Write On!

Writing verses down on note cards, in a small notebook, or using the 'sticky note' function of your tablet, laptop, or phone, is how some people memorize best. Writing the verses down requires you to look at them and think about what you are writing. In some ways, this method makes the verses more real—not just words you read on a page.

Writing the verses down gives you the ability to take them with you everywhere you go; meaning you can look at them and work on memorizing them anytime and anywhere. If you write the verses you want to memorize on notecards, you can put them on:

- Your mirror
- Cabinet of closet doors

- In your Bible to be part of your daily Bible study
- On the treadmill so you can memorize and walk at the same time
- By the TV remote to remind you of what is really important
- On your pillow or on your nightstand to say before you go to bed each night
- By the coffee maker so you can work on them while you enjoy your morning coffee
- On the dashboard of your car

Some people who memorize best by writing verses keep a notebook—virtual or hard copy—in which they write the verses they are memorizing over and over...and over again. In doing so they are able to remember the verses because they have to put focused thought on what they are writing.

As for putting them on your phone or computer, I think it's safe to say you will rarely be more than an arm's reach away from these things, so you will have plenty of opportunities to stop what you are doing for a few minutes several times a day to work on memorizing God's Word. Remember, though, you have to make and take those opportunities in order for them to produce results.

I sent myself an email from one account to another. It listed several of the verses I want to memorize. Every time I check my email, I take a few minutes to read that one, too. I say the verses I've already memorized so I don't forget them, and then work on the next one. Sometimes I say them out loud and other times I say them to myself—depending on where I am. This might not work for everyone, but it's worked for me. ~Dave

Once you have a verse or verses memorized, you can also ask someone to test or quiz you on what you've learned. This proved to be highly effective in the study group Darla was in...

We used notecards in our group. On one side we wrote the verse and where it is found and on the other side we only wrote where the verse was found. We would quiz each other by holding up the side of the card with the scripture references and our partner would have to say the verse. It was a great way to learn.

If you are unsure of how Darla's group's flashcard system worked, look at the example that follows to help you better understand it.

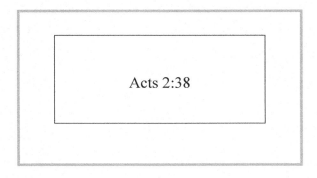

> Repent and be baptized , every one of you in the name of Jesus Christ for the forgiveness of your sins and you will receive the gift of the Holy Spirit. Acts 2:38

I realize some of you may not have the blessing of having others to study and memorize with or the time to do so on a regular basis. Sometimes life requires us to set our study time late at night or early in the morning when we have a bit of quiet time to ourselves—

neither being conducive to studying with a group.

If this is the case, you can still use the flashcard system—it just might not be quite as much fun doing it by yourself as it is doing it with a group of your brothers and sisters in Christ.

NOTE: The flashcard system is also a great way for families to work together to commit Bible verses to memory. School-age children are familiar with this form of learning and usually pick it up quite easily.

Let your artistic side show through

No one said memorizing Bible verses was supposed to be boring. When making your notecards or notes on your phone or computer, get creative! Use bright-colored markers and paper or cards. There are lots of options out there so don't think you have to settle for boring old white cards or even the neon-colored ones if that isn't your 'thing'.

You can use a journal or create a SMASH book of Bible verses—complete with doodles, drawings, stickers or whatever you want to add.

Use different fonts to emphasize words or phrases in a verse you are having trouble with to help them stand out. Use fonts that are fun to look at—ones that remind you of the doodling you did when you were a kid.

If you write out your cards, write them out in your best handwriting. This small, seemingly unimportant gesture makes you focus on what is being written and subconsciously retains at least a portion of it. Your neatness also validates the fact that God's Word is worth your best effort.

The Israelites were instructed by Moses to make the Law a prominent part of their lives.

He told them to talk about it, bind it to their foreheads, and make it visible in their homes (Deuteronomy 6:4-9). We're no longer under the Law of Moses, but these verses can and should still apply to us today in regards to both the Old and New Testaments.

More Than Just Words on a Page

So far we've given you several practical ways to help you memorize scripture, but now I think it's time we talk about the 'why' of memorizing and how to prepare your heart and your mind for what you are doing.

Why you need to memorize Bible verses

Aside from the obvious fact that memorizing verses from the Bible makes you more sure of who you are as a Christian and what God expects from his children, there are several important reasons for memorizing scripture.

- The Holy Spirit will bring these words to mind when you need comfort, strength, encouragement, and want to share your joy, thankfulness, and excitement with the LORD.
- You will be better equipped to share your faith with others.
- You will be better equipped to defend your faith and beliefs when others question or persecute you.
- Knowing God's Word provides a strong foundation for making Godly choices and decisions rather than listening to the worldview of things.
- As a Christian it is essential that you know why you believe what you believe and that you know what God wants and expects from you.

How to memorize

We've already covered some of the methods of memorizing verses from the Bible, but all the pretty notecards and the most dedicated group members in the world won't be beneficial if you don't prepare yourself for this spiritual journey. Unless you commit your heart and mind to putting God's Word into your heart and mind, your efforts will not be fruitful.

First of all, you have to get rid of the attitude that says "I can't". If you believe you can't, you won't.

Secondly your heart needs to be in the right place. You have to *want* to know God's Word in order for it to really take hold. Memorizing for the sake of memorizing or because you want others to see you as a Bible scholar may help you learn the words, but you won't have the meaning of those words in your heart. They won't change your attitudes, actions, and thought processes. Remember...the purest motives produce the greatest (and purest) results.

In order to get your heart and mind in the right place, take a few minutes before you begin to read and study to **pray**; asking God to open your heart and mind to the meaning of what you are reading and working to memorize, and to give you the ability to imprint those words on your heart and mind forever.

When you read a verse to memorize it, **read the verse in context.** This is very important, as it almost always makes the meaning more clear and makes it easy to remember/memorize. Why? Because you are memorizing a thought...a command from God...words of wisdom, comfort, or instruction for God rather than a few sentences.

Most Bibles will have headings or titles at the beginning of a section of scripture (within the chapter). It will be helpful for you to read several verses before and after the verse you are memorizing to get the full meaning of what is being said. Otherwise, you may have a more difficult time understanding what you are reading and memorizing, or even more critical, you may mistake the message. If this would be the case, not only would you be misguided, but you might also give others the wrong message when sharing the Word with them. For example, look at the following verse found in Ecclesiastes 2:17:

So I hated life, because the work that is done under the sun was grievous to me. All of it is meaningless, a chasing after the wind.

If you were to simply memorize that verse, you would get the impression that life here on earth isn't meant to be enjoyed and that it's useless to take joy in what you do. Right? But if you read the verse in *context*, you find that

Solomon is warning us that life is about much more than worldly pleasures and materialism. He's saying that in comparison to what happens when we die, these things are worthless and meaningless, and that our focus should be on living a life here that will leave a Godly legacy with those who come after us and that will give us the hope of eternity with God.

That's quite a difference, isn't it?

I think it is safe to say this would never be an intentional act on your part, so please take the time to be sure you get the context and true meaning of what is being said before memorizing a verse.

The Bible you use should be a translation rather than a version of the Bible. So what's the difference?

TRANSLATION: A literal conversion of the original text from the Hebrew, Greek and

Aramaic languages spoken at the time of the writing by the authors of the Bible. The King James was the first translation and uses 'thou' 'shall' 'shalt', 'thee' 'thy' and 'thine' quite often. There is nothing wrong with that and it is correct. The NIV translation, which came later, has replaced those words with 'you', 'will', 'should' 'your' and other grammatically and translationally correct pronouns.

NOTE: I know that NIV stands for New International Version, which seems to present itself as an oxymoron, of sorts, but rest assured that the NIV is a translation rather than a version of the Bible.

VERSION: An interpretation of a translation of the Bible by a single person or group of people for the intended purpose of making the Bible easier to understand. Now while that may sound like a great and even sensible idea, it doesn't always work out that way. The writers of the various versions of the Bible are not:

- Using the original Hebrew, Greek, and Aramaic text
- As concerned about literal translation of the Word as they are in digestible (easily understood) presentation
- Accurate

That last one (accurate) may make some of you uneasy and leave you wondering how or why these versions of the Bible would be inaccurate, so let's talk briefly about it before we go on.

HOW: The fact that the writers of the many different versions of the Bible are not using original text leaves lots of room for error. This can be coupled with the fact that the purpose in putting these versions out there is to make the

Bible more appealing or easy for people. This takes us to the 'why'.

WHY: Jesus plainly tells us that he is the way, truth, and light and that the only way to the Father God is through him. I don't know about you, but I don't think it gets much plainer than that. Even a small child can understand this statement and the fact that obedience to Jesus is what it takes to be with God.

The trouble with this is that even though it is simple to understand, it's not always as simple to do it. Why? We don't want to give up our sinful lifestyles. We don't want to give back to God what he gave us in the first place. We don't want to be made to feel guilty for not serving in our church, being pure until our wedding night, faithful to our spouse, gossiping about anyone and everyone, lying, cheating on our taxes, partying and getting drunk, treating others rudely, and all those other things Jesus says cannot be a part of who we are when we are with him. So...the versions of the Bible water down the truth of God's Word. They make it easier to go along with because the way many of them are written don't make us nearly as uncomfortable. For example, in 1st Corinthians 6 the NIV *translation* says:

Or do you not know that wrongdoers will not inherit the kingdom of God? Do not be deceived: Neither the sexually immoral nor idolaters nor adulterers nor men who have sex with men nor thieves nor the greedy nor drunkards nor slanderers nor swindlers will inherit the kingdom of God. ~1st Corinthians 6:9-10

Now look at these same verses as written in The Message...a loose *version* of the Bible.

Don't you realize that this is not the way to live? Unjust people who don't care about God will not be joining in his kingdom. Those who use and abuse each other, use and abuse sex, use and abuse the earth and everything in it, don't qualify as citizens in God's kingdom.

That's quite a difference, don't you agree? The Message leaves it wide open for the reader to decide what his or her definition of abusing each other, abusing sex, or abusing the earth is. These are not things that have been left for us to decide—these are things God decided. We only have the right to choose whether or not we want to obey him.

All that being said, I will say that not all versions are as loosely written, nor is it wrong or bad to have a version of the Bible to look at for comparison when studying the Bible. Children's Bibles are another exception to this rule. Toddlers and preschoolers are blessed to have a variety of beautiful picture story Bibles that introduce them to the power and glory of God and his son, Jesus. But to use a version rather than a translation as your sole source of Bible study and for memorization is not wise.

Using the translated text is ALWAYS better than using someone's idea of what the verse means.

A Great Place to Start

When you learned to walk you learned to put one foot in front of the other; taking one step at a time. When you learned to drive, your confidence behind the wheel came as you got some miles under your belt. You also had to learn that two plus two equals four long before you knew that four times four equals sixteen or that A minus B is equal to C times five. The point? Memorizing scripture doesn't have to be done with lightning speed or in great quantities. It isn't how many verses you memorize, but how well you know and understand the ones you memorize.

The following is a list of scriptures that are especially meaningful to Christians and to those who are searching to know God. Yes, the list is long. Don't let that discourage or frighten you. By no means do you have to learn them all or learn any of them overnight. Read through them. Mark the three you would like to learn first. Once you have memorized those three, you can move on to the next three...then the next...and the next.... But remember to keep those you've already learned fresh in your mind by saying them at least three or four times a week.

If this is all new to you, I know it sounds daunting, but it isn't. God can and will give you the knowledge and wisdom to memorize his Word. You just have to ask for it and then take it. If you do, I guarantee the verses you learn will soon be as deeply planted in your mind as the "Happy Birthday" song, your child's birthday, or the password to your email account.

NOTE: The verses are in no particular order of importance.

Genesis 1:1 "In the beginning God created the heavens and the earth."

Joshua 1:8 "Do not let this Book of the Law depart from your mouth; meditate on it day and night, so that you may be careful to do everything written in it."

Exodus 4:11-12 "The LORD said to him, "Who gave man his mouth? Who makes him deaf or mute? Who gives him sight or makes him blind? Is it not I, the LORD? Now go; I will help you speak and will teach you what to say."

Exodus 14:14 "The LORD will fight for you; you need only to be still."

Exodus 20:1-17 "And God spoke all these words: "I am the LORD your God, who brought you out of Egypt, out of the land of slavery. You shall have no other gods before me. You shall not make for yourself an idol in the form of anything in heaven above or on the earth beneath or in the waters below. Yu shall not bow down to them or worship them; for I the LORD your God am a jealous God, punishing the children for the sin of the fathers to the third and fourth generation of those who hate me, but showing love to a thousand generations of those who love me and keep my commandments. You shall not misuse the name of the LORD your God, for the LORD will not hold anyone guiltless who misuses his name. Remember the Sabbath day by keeping it holy. Six days you shall labor and do all your work, but the seventh day is a Sabbath to the LORD your God. On it you shall not do any work, neither you, nor your son or daughter, nor your manservant or maidservant, nor your animals, nor the alien within your gates. For in six days the LORD made the heavens and the earth, the sea and all that is in them, but he rested on the seventh day. Therefore the LORD blessed the Sabbath day and made it holy.

Honor your father and your mother, so that you may live long in the land the LORD your God is giving you. You shall not murder. You shall not commit adultery. You shall not steal. You shall not give false testimony against your neighbor. You shall not covet your neighbor's house. You shall not covet your neighbor's wife, or his manservants or maidservant, his ox, or donkey or anything that belongs to your neighbor."

1st Samuel 2:2 "There is no one holy like the LORD; there is no one besides you; there is no Rock like our God."

1st Samuel 16:7 "But the LORD said o Samuel, "Do not consider his appearance or his height for I have rejected him. The LORD does not look at the things man looks at. Man looks at the outward appearance, but the LORD looks at the heart."

2nd Samuel 24:24 "But the King replied to Araunah, "No, I insist on paying you for it. I will not sacrifice to the LORD my God burnt offerings that cost me nothing."

2nd Chronicles 7:14 "If my people, who are called by my name, will humble themselves and pray and seek my face and turn from their wicked ways, then will I hear from heaven and will forgive their sin and will heal their land."

Esther 4:14 "For if you remain silent at this time, relief and deliverance for the Jews will arise from another place, but you and your father's family will perish. And who knows but that you have come to royal position for such a time as this?"

Job 4:17-18 "Blessed is the man whom God corrects, so do not despise the discipline of the Almighty. For he wounds, but he also binds up, he injures, but his hands also heal."

Job 22:20 "Submit to God and be at peace with him; in this way prosperity will come to you."

Job 32:9 "It is not only the old who are wise, not only the aged who understand what is right."

Job 33:14 "For God does speak—now one way, now another—though man may not perceive it."

Psalm 1: "Bless is the man who does not walk in the counsel of the wicked or stand in the way of sinners or sit in the seat of mockers. But his delight is in the law of the LORD, and on his law he meditates day and night. He is like a tree planted by streams of water, which yields its fruit in season and whose leaf does not wither. Whatever he does prospers. Not so the wicked! They are like chaff that the wind blows away. Therefore the wicked will not stand in the judgement, nor sinners in the assembly of the righteous. For the LORD watches over the way of the righteous, but the way of the wicked will perish."

Psalm 5:3 "In the morning, O LORD, you hear my voice; in the morning I lay my requests before you and wit in expectation."

Psalm 9:10 "Those who know your name will trust in you, for you, LORD< have never forsaken those who seek you."

Psalm 16:5-6 "LORD, you have assigned me my portion and my cup, you have made my lot secure. The boundary lines have fallen for me in pleasant places; surely I have a delightful inheritance."

Psalm 19:14 "May the words of my mouth and the meditation of my heart be pleasing in your sight, O LORD, my Rock and my Redeemer."

Psalm 33: 4 "For the word of the LORD is right and true; he is faithful in all he does."

Psalm 37:4 "Delight yourself in the LORD and he will give you the desires of your heart."

Psalm 119:133 "Direct my footsteps according to your word; let no sin rule over me."

Psalm 133:1 "How good and pleasant it is when brothers live together in unity."

Psalm 139:14 "I praise you because I am fearfully and wonderfully made; your works are wonderful, I know that full well."

Proverbs 1:7 "The fear of the LORD is the beginning of knowledge, but fools despise wisdom and discipline."

Proverbs 4:23 "Above all else, guard your heart, for it is the wellspring of life."

Proverbs 6:16-19 "There are six things the LORD hates, seven that are detestable to him: haughty eyes, a lying tongue, hands hat shed innocent blood, a heart the devises wicked schemes, feet that are quick to rush into evil, a false witness who pours out lies and a man who stirs up dissention among brothers."

Proverbs 11:4 "Wealth is worthless in the day of wrath, but righteousness delivers from death."

Proverbs 16:1 "To man belong the plans of the heart, but from the LORD comes the reply of the tongue."

Proverbs 16:3 "Commit to the LORD whatever you do, and your plans will succeed."

Proverbs 17:1 "Better a dry crust with peace and quiet than a house full of feasting with strife."

Proverbs 19:21 "Many are the plans in a man's heart, but it is the LORD's purpose that prevails."

Ecclesiastes 3:1-8 "There is a time for everything, and a season for everything activity under heaven: a time to be born and a time to die, a time to plant and a time to uproot, a time to kill and a time to heal, a time to tear down and a time to build, a time to weep and a time to laugh, a time to mourn and a time to dance, a time to scatter stones and a time to gather them, a time to embrace and a time to refrain, a time to search and a time to give up, a time to keep and a time to throw away, a time to tear and a time to mend, a time to be silent and a time to speak, a time to love and a time to hate, a time for war and a time for peace."

Ecclesiastes 4:10 "If one falls down, his friend can help him up. But pity the man who falls and has no one to help him up."

Ecclesiastes 7:1 "A good name is better than fine perfume, and the day of death better than the day of birth."

Ecclesiastes 11:9 "Be happy, young many, while you are young and let your heart give you joy in the days of your youth. Follow the ways of your heart and whatever your eyes see, but know that for all these things God will bring you to judgement."

Ecclesiastes 12: 13-14 "Now all has been heard; here is the conclusion of the matter: Fear God and keep his commandments, for this is the whole duty of man. For God will bring every deed into judgment, including every hidden thing, whether it is good or evil."

Isaiah 40:8 "The grass withers and the flowers fall, but the word of our God stands forever."

Isaiah 40:28 "Do you not know? Have you not heard? The LORD is the everlasting God, the Creator of the ends of the earth. He will not grow tired or weary, and his understanding no one can fathom."

Isaiah 59:1 "Surely the arm of the LORD is not too short to save, nor his ear too dull to hear."

Jeremiah 29:11-13 "For I know the plans I have for you, declares the LORD, plans to prosper you and not to harm you, plans to give you hope and a future. Then you will call upon me and come and pray to me, and I will listen to you. You will seek me and find me when you seek me with all your heart."

Matthew 5:3-10 "Blessed are the poor in spirit, for theirs is the kingdom of heaven. Blessed are those who mourn, for they will be comforted. Blessed are the meek, for they will inherit the earth. Blessed are those who hunger and thirst for righteousness, for they will be filled. Blessed are the merciful, for they will be shown mercy. Blessed are the pure in heart, for they will see God. Blessed are the peacemakers, for they will be called the sons of God. Blessed are those who are persecuted because of righteousness, for theirs in the kingdom of heaven."

Matthew 6:9-15 "This, then, is how you should pray: Our Father in heaven, hallowed be your name, your kingdom come, your will be done on earth as it is in heaven. Give us today our daily bread. Forgive us our debts, as we also have forgiven our debtors. And lead us not into temptation, but deliver us from the evil one. For if you forgive men when they sin against you, your heavenly Father will also forgive you. But if you do not forgive men their sins, your Father will not forgive your sins."

Matthew 7:12 "So in everything, do to others what you would have them do to you, for this sums up the Law and the Prophets."

Matthew 10:32-33 "Whoever acknowledges me before men, I will also acknowledge him before my Father in heaven. But whoever disowns me before men, I will disown him before my Father in heaven."

Matthew 16:16 "Simon Peter answered, "You are the Christ, the Son of the living God."

Matthew 24:35 "Heaven and earth will pass away, but my words will never pass away."

Matthew 28:18-20 "Then Jesus came to them and said, "All authority in heaven and on earth has been give tome. Therefore, go and make disciples of all nations, baptizing them in the name of the Father and of the Son and of the Holy Spirit, and teaching them to obey everything I have commanded you. And surely

I am with you always to the very end of the age.""

Mark 3:16-18 "These are the twelve he appointed: Simon (to whom he gave the name Peter); James son of Zebedee and his brother John (to them he gave the name Boanerges, which means Sons of Thunder); Andrew, Philip, Bartholomew, Matthew, Thomas, James son of Alphaeus, Thaddaeus, Simon the Zealot and Judas Iscariot, who betrayed him."

Mark 14: 22-24 "While they were eating, Jesus took bread, gave thanks and broke it and gave it to his disciples, saying, "Take it; this is my body." Then he took the cup, gave thanks and offered it to them, and they all drank from it. "This is my blood of the covenant, which is poured out for many," he said to them."

Mark 16:16 "Whoever believes and is baptized will be saved, but whoever does not believe will be condemned."

Luke 1:37 "For nothing is impossible with God."

Luke 23:46 "Then Jesus called out with a loud voice, "Father, into your hands I commit my spirit." When had said this, he breathed his last."

John 1:1 "In the beginning was the Word, and the Word was with God, and the Word was God."

John 3:5 "Jesus answered, "I tell you the truth, no can enter the kingdom of God unless he is born of water and the Spirit."

John 3:16 "For God so loved the world that he gave his one and only Son, that whoever believes in him shall not perish but have eternal life."

John 14:6 "Jesus answered, "I am the way and the truth and the life. No one come to the Father except through me."

Acts 2:38 "Peter replied, "Repent and be baptized, every one of you, in the name of Jesus Christ for the forgiveness of your sins. And you will receive the gift of the Holy Spirit."

Acts 22:16 "And now what are you waiting for? Get up, be baptized and wash your sins away, calling on his name."

Romans 1:16 "I am not ashamed of the gospel, because it is the power of God for the salvation of everyone who believers: first for the Jew, then for the Gentile."

Romans 2:6 "God will give to each person according to what he has done."

Romans 3:23-24 "For all have sinned and fall short of the glory of God, and are justified freely by his grace through the redemption that came by Christ Jesus."

Romans 5:8 "But God demonstrates his own love for us in this: While we were still sinners, Christ died for us."

Romans 6:1-2 "What shall we say, then? Shall we go on sinning so that grace may increase? By no means! We died to sin; how can we live in it any longer?"

Romans 6:23 "For the wages of sin is death but the gift of God is sternal lie in Christ Jesus our LORD."

Romans 8:28: "And we know that in all things God works for the good of those who love him, who have been called according to his purpose."

Romans 12:1 "Therefore, I urge you, brothers, in view of God's mercy, to offer your bodies as living sacrifices, holy and pleasing to God—this is your spiritual act of worship."

Romans 12:9 "Love must be sincere. Hate what is evil; cling to what is good."

Romans 13:1 "Everyone must submit himself to the governing authorities, for there is no authority except that which God has established. The authorities that exist have been established by God."

1st Corinthians 10:13 "No temptation has seized you except what is common to man. And God is faithful; he will not let you be tempted beyond what you can bear. But when you are tempted, he will provide a way out so that you can stand up under it."

1st Corinthians 13:4-7 "Love is patent, love is kind It does not envy, it does not boast, it is not proud. It is not rude, it is not self-seeking, I is not easily angered, it keeps no record of wrongs, Love does not delight in evil but rejoices with the truth. It always projects, always trusts, always hopes, always perseveres.

1st Corinthians 15:33 "Do not be misled: "Bad company corrupts good character".

2nd Corinthians 9:6-7 "Remember this: Whoever sows sparingly will also reap sparingly, and whoever sows generously will also reap generously. Each man should give what he has decided in his heart to give, not reluctantly or under compulsion, for God loves a cheerful giver."

Galatians 3:27 "For all of you who were baptized into Christ have clothed yourselves with Christ."

Galatians 5:22-23 "But the fruit of the Spirit is loe, joy, peace, patience, kindness, goodness, faithfulness, gentleness and self-control. Against such things there is no law."

Ephesians 4:4-6 "There is one body and one Spirit—just as you were called to one hope when you were called—one LORD, one faith, one baptism: one God and Father of all who is over all and through all and in all."

Ephesians 6:7 "Serve wholeheartedly, as if you were serving LORD, not men."

Philippians 2:14-15 "Do everything without complaining or arguing, so that you maybe come blameless and pure, children of God without fault in a crooked and depraved generation, in which you shine like stars in the universe."

Philippians 4:6-7 "Do not be anxious about anything, but in everything, by prayer and petition, with thanksgiving, present your requests to God. And the peace of God, which transcends all understanding, will guard your hearts and your minds in Christ Jesus."

1st Thessalonians 5:16-18 "Be joyful always, pray continually; give thanks in all circumstances, for this is God's will for you in Christ Jesus."

1st Timothy 4:12 "Don't let anyone look down on you because you are young, but set an example for the believers in speech, in life, in love, in faith and in purity."

Hebrews 10:23 "Let us hold unswervingly to the hlpe we profess, for he who promised is faithful."

Hebrews 10:26-27 "If we deliberately keep on sinning after we have received the knowledge of the truth, no sacrifice for sins is left, but only a fearful expectation of judgement and the raging fire that will consume the enemies of God."

Hebrews 11:6 "And without faith it is impossible to please God, because anyone who comes to him must believe that he exists and that he reward those who earnestly seek him."

Hebrews 12:7 "Endure hardship as discipline; God is treating you as sons. For what son is not disciplined by his father?"

Hebrews 13:7 "Remember your leaders who spoke the word of God to you. Consider the outcome of their way of life and imitate their faith.

Hebrews 13:8 "Jesus Christ is the same yesterday and today and forever."

James 1:19 "My dear brothers, take note of this: Everyone should be quick to listen, slow to speak, and slow to become angry."

James 3:17 "But the wisdom that comes from heaven is first of all pure; then peace-loving, considerate, submissive, full of mercy and good fruit, impartial and sincere."

1st Peter 3:15 "But in your hearts set apart Christ as LORD. Always be prepared to give an answer to everyone who asks you to give the reason for the hop that you have. But do this with gentleness and respect."

1st Peter 5:6-7 "Humble yourselves, therefore, under God's mighty hand, that he may lift you up in due time. Cast all your anxiety on him because he cares for you."

1st John 1:8-9 "If we claim to be without sin, we deceive ourselves and the truth is not in us. If we confess our sins, he is faithful and just and will forgive us our sins and purify us from all unrighteousness."

1st John 2:6 "Whoever claims to live in him must walk as Jesus did."

1st John 2:17 "The world and its desires pass away, but the man who does the will of God lives forever."

1st John 3:16 "This is how we know what love is: Jesus Christ laid down his life for us. And we ought to lay down our lives for our brothers."

1st John 3:18 "dear children, let us not love with words or tongue but with actions and in truth."

Additional Resources

Often times we seek out comfort, instruction, and encouragement from the Bible for particular life situations we are dealing with. When we are grieving, we long to hear words of comfort and hope. When we are worried about our parenting skills we want reassurance and instruction on how God desires us to parent. When we are angry we want answers on how to deal with that anger. When we...(fill in the blank).

The following websites are extremely helpful in guiding you to where you need to go at times like these (and many other). But remember...don't just read. Put God's words in your heart and mind so that they are there 24/7. There are also websites to resources for fun and memorizing tools to help you on your way.

- www.biblegateway.com
- www.openbible.info
- http://www.cafepress.com/+cute+journals
- www.hobbylobby.com

Your Free Gift:

Thanks for reading my book and as a way of saying Thank You I have this free gift for you.

In Bible Verses and Inspirational Christian Quotes Book , you will have quotes and explanations some very important aspects of our life i.e Friendship, Life, Peace, Motivation, Salvation and many more...

You can check this link for getting your free gift: ***http://briangugas.com/free-gift***

BRIAN GUGAS

Other Books By Brian

Book1

Bible Study Guide for Beginners: Each of the 66 books explained for Getting Started.

Link: *http://www.amazon.com/Bible-Study-Guide-Beginners-Brian-ebook/dp/B00MUFP1QG*

Book2

How to Study The Bible: Study guide on How and where to Start learning The Bible

Link: http://www.amazon.com/How-Study-Bible-Beginners-Learning-ebook/dp/B013OGDVLG

You can also **check my Author link** here to get the complete list of books

Link: **http://briangugas.com/author**

BRIAN GUGAS